THE LITTLE HOUSE ON STILTS REMEMBERS

Poems

Naomi Ruth Lowinsky

Blue Light Press

WINNER OF THE *2014 BLUE LIGHT POETRY PRIZE*

THE LITTLE HOUSE ON STILTS REMEMBERS

Copyright © 2015 by **Naomi Ruth Lowinsky**

Printed in the United States of America

BOOK AND COVER DESIGN
Melanie Gendron
www.melaniegendron.com

COVER ART
"Little House on Stilts" by Melanie Gendron

AUTHOR PHOTO
Nora Lowinsky

ISBN: 978-1-4218-3737-6

FIRST PRINTING

BLUE LIGHT PRESS
www.bluelightpress.com
Email: bluelightpress@aol.com

ACKNOWLEDGEMENTS

M any thanks to the editors of the following publications in which some of these poems have appeared, often in earlier versions:

Angel Face: "Flesh Gates" "Lament of the House"

The Book of Now: Poetry for the Rising Tide: "Where Coyote Brush Roams"

Cadillac Cicatrix: "Thunder   My Love"

California Quarterly: "Wet Lands"

Child of My Child: Anthology: "In the Garden"

GW: "Madonna   My Dove"

Jewish Women's Literary Annual: "To an Old Man from Bosnia"

The Pinch: "Many Houses Ago" (first section)

Poem: "Her Next Life"

Weber Studies: "Doorway Dream," "At the Inn of Placelessness," and "Wild Girl of Pleasant Hill"

Willow Review: "It's Because of the Storm"

TABLE OF CONTENTS

for Nelly Sachs,

who saw the light, even in exile

and for Dan

who makes our house home

HER NEXT LIFE

All the houses she's loved and sold
remember her
call her by name

What will her next life be?

In the dream she must change
clothes   stitch mirrors
red thread
on deer skin dress
            reflect her
            journey   temple dancer
                stone chariot
                river at sunset with elephants

All the pretty houses have peeled off
                            like snake skin

Her feet are listening
            Song of the earth
                        holds her now

MADONNA   MY DOVE

How do you come by your calm
you of the sepia breast?
It's been weeks on those eggs
in that nest

Don't cars roar past?
Isn't the air exhausted?
Aren't the trees breathing fumes?
Don't I go clamoring in and out
full of my noisy thoughts   startling you
with a great flap of wings
out of the question mark tree?

How do you get back your calm?
Do you watch your thoughts?
Slow down your breath?
Do you hear the song
of your mother's mother
pressing your breast
against the soon
              to be seen?

Will they be twisted and sick
Will they be graceful and swift
              Messiahs of the olive branch
              Hatchlings
                    of the question mark tree?

FLESH GATES

When it is time I will leave
this house of light   Hawk
has flown over me   Eagle
watched me
from the power pole   Deer halted me

on the road   Wisteria glowed
through my kitchen window   Squirrel
observed me make tea   Mad bird
flew into his reflection
over and over again   Blue jay

pecked holes in my roof   Words visited
and gods who are blazes
of fire   I sat
on this wooden porch and saw
the poplar cut down   yellow flame

of its tongue   severed   and knew
like the white mist
that tucks itself into the corners
of the valley   like the red
tailed hawk that soars toward the western hills

I will be gone
cut loose
from these breasts
these thighs
                    shattered
                    like the wine glass at the wedding

gone home

to what was mine
before I passed
      through flesh gates
           into Mother's arms

It's Because of the Storm

how the rain leaks in
how it gets under the skin of the house
past wood   past glass   how it drips
on the circular stair   that whatever faith

I have about haven   leaks
away   Wind is a wild
animal   It claws through
my mind   lets in the banshee

shriekers   the bone rattlers   the howlers   One
who has made of his body a bomb   is in pieces
among pieces of others   in the news
of that war that won't end

Sometimes a shift in the wind
brings me the song my grandmother sang
of a storm and a galloping horse
a child in the presence of death   His father

will not comprehend   Death is about
to touch him   icicle hands   Death is
the valley in winter   ghosts
that complain

they died too young   Dead branch
claws at my window   must be
some spirit who wants my life
                              knows my name

LAMENT OF THE HOUSE

Haven't I stroked you with fingers of light?
Haven't I gentled your eyes?
Haven't I filled you to brimming
with the green world?   How it goes
golden and brown   How it loses

its leaves and goes bare?   Haven't I shown you
the setting sun   streaked
purple and orange
while white fog   like sea foam
flows over the western hills?

Haven't you stood on my deck
poured red wine on the earth
said praises?   Haven't I held
your clay goddesses   your dancing
Ganesha   your Zuni frogs?

How can you tear me apart   empty me out
get me staged to be god knows whose
fantasy house on a ridge?   I who've been source
of your source   sacred seat
as clouds form   hawks dive

Haven't you sat   on that old yellow chair   visited
by poetry?   Haven't you stood in me   naked
in the gaze of the great horned one?
Will you send your gods into exile
in cardboard boxes?   Will the soles of your feet be gone
                                        from my spiral stairs?

Where will your enthusiasms go   your wrestling
angels   your love cries?   "Nasty" you called me
when I thrust that redwood splinter under your nail
How else can I say it?   You and I

                              are inside one another

PRAYER

Come to me
though my house is no longer my house
though my name has been lost in the mails
though dangerous strangers lurk

Come to me
though my basket is empty
though the hills have forgotten my gaze
and the moon is losing her grip

Where are you who woke me at night
who stared with raptor eyes
filled my skull with first light?

Come to me
though I don't know the way
through painted slats
over concrete stairs

Come to me
though the news is terrible
every day somebody's son
blows himself up to make somebody's
father   somebody's mother and child
body parts in the market

Come to me
though I've lost my grandmother's thread
though my words have forgotten their roots

Surely
if agapanthus reach out purple fingers
if willows drape their hair
if an egret
        lifts great wings

                        you
                        must be here

Many Houses Ago

1.
I wish I could see
those fabled houses from before I was born
home of my grandparents in the hills above Kassel
home of the poet Nelly Sachs on Lessingstrasse in Berlin

the crystal   the silver fish knives   the music room   the library
the well-tempered Bach   the Hölderin   the Goethe
Buber's "Legend
of the Baal Shem Tov" who it is said

                                        ascended
                                        to the radiance

We wander around America
transporting what's left
from haunted house
to haunted house

the house with the pond and the scary catfish
the house with the frieze of dancing maenads
the house on the ridge where we watched the sun circle
from summer to winter and back

Always I am also
in that other life
the Nazis have confiscated home
Nelly Sachs has made it to sanctuary
sits in a white room in Stockholm
talking to stones

"O the chimneys
. . . cleverly devised houses of death
when Israel's body dissolves
into smoke."

2.
"This is an excursion into a place
where the shadows sign other contracts,"
wrote Nelly   So it seemed to me until
many houses ago   Dan arrived

We lay together
on a mattress on the floor
home at last
in our creature bodies

home for his children   my children   How many
for dinner?   Vegetable chopping   garlic peeling
laughter at table   Whose turn
to do the dishes?

Meanwhile in my other life
Nelly is writing a letter
to Paul Celan
He discovered her

"Chorus of the Orphans" her
"Chorus of the Stones" in a French journal
"Blessed by Bach and Hölderin   writes Nellie
 Blessed by Hasidim"

3.
Before I read your lamentations Nelly
to the "earth ... gone blind"
before I read your "lioness of pain"   I knew

that lioness   My grandmother
born in Berlin in 1881   like you   orphaned
by the axe   "kindling in a woodcutter's hand"

She with her paintbrush
of shadow and light
You with your language of stones

I sit in my study   entranced
by my grandmother's painting
a radiant lake   a mountain lost

in mist   entranced
by your "glowing enigmas"   so beautiful
in German   "Die Glühende Rätsel"   Nelly I know

your Zohar   your "alphabet angel"
and sometimes   unbidden
that light   Paul saw it

the time you visited
in Paris   He kept waiting
to see it again   poor Paul

who had slammed out of his house in Bukovina
in 1942 and never
saw his parents again   You who talk

to the dead and are afraid of what
knocks on the pipes   survive
for Paul's next letter

for the "gold to appear
        out of the mystery."

4.
It's not about the houses
it's the husband
who makes it home
He who feeds the birds

12

keeps the fountain flowing   tends tomatoes
He of the kind shoulders   the little boy
murmurings   yabadaba dooba
oobee doobee da

We've made so many homes together
not one has been Jerusalem
When the mountain climbed into my study
one winter morning

I thought of you   Nelly
living my other life

5.
Ah Nelly   the horrors have not stopped
since Paul slipped into the Seine
in April 1970   since you slipped away
soon after   Terror has a closet full

of new clothes   Beware
of the fierce ones on horseback   Beware
of the silent ones
wearing bombs

The women who squat
in refugee camps
feed their children stories of home   where once
there was a glimpse of the radiance

Nelly we sat in the garden
of our latest home   me and my Dan
on a warm May Sunday   Bach in the air   visitations
by golden finches   He said to me   blowing a kiss

"Isn't this fun?"

If he leaves me for the world to come   will I crawl
into this moment   make it my
lost home?   Or will I climb into bed with you   Nelly

listen to what knocks on the water pipes
listen to stones
Will we wander
into the invisible temple

Will we meet the Baal Shem Tov?

Doorway Dream

The woman in my dream is naked   She seems
some sort of wood nymph   no longer young   but radiant
as trees in the sun   She sits on the ground
a green plant grows out of her spine   Its leaves
are hands   They bless

the crown of her head   This is
the very plant by the door
of the townhouse Dan and I just bought
from a young Bosnian   whose father Mohammed said
"One leaf dies   Three more grow!"

He showed us the grapevine he had planted
the persimmon   the yellow rose
The middle aged wood nymph has no patience
for lamentations about lost houses
lovely valley views   She says

Consider the roses   When Leah showed Dan
how to prune   she cut just above
each nascent bloom
You've been cut back   here
in the garden of Mohammed

To an Old Man from Bosnia

I never expected persimmons
That tree you planted
before this became our home

was a stick in the winter mud
Your name   you said   was Mohammed
I wonder what lies behind you

You tended your son's garden
What he loved was
fast cars

It's been three times September
since we bought this home
That scrawny tree surprised us

clusters of hard green fruit   turning gold
I'd not known persimmons
their taste from another world

the splendor they steal from the sun
I wish we could talk
We'd walk in the garden

admire your plantings
I've been wanting to tell you   Mohammed
I never expected persimmons

Thunder My Love

Your eyes are caves
where wild cats
sleep   Honey suckle
the smell of us   The bed sails
to an island
                    mangos and papayas

Moon drops in
through sky light
Coyotes yip yap
You're on the road
to Baghdad
                    carrying too much
                              baggage

There is no empty drawer
in this house   your socks
my Indian shawls   our purple
blanket   You roll over
in the night   Our hands
remember   sanctuaries
                    of flesh

Roses climb all over
the back fence   even
in our sleep   wind chimes   news
of the war   Baghdad has fallen
                              again

Which of us is quaking
aspen   Which of us is
lightening bolt

17

Thunder my love   among trees

rain fall

rain

fall

WHERE COYOTE BRUSH ROAMS

Well they'd made up their minds to be everywhere because why not.
—W.S. Merwin

We were high on the sky when we lived on that ridge   high
on the red tailed hawk   high
on the long green rumps of the hills going yellow
while the sun did its dance from winter to summer and back
                  high
on our ridge after work while the fog flowed over
darkening hills   We poured red wine on the earth   high
on escape from the city's exhaust   high
on the song of the frogs in the pond
some man had made
Never mind

that the pines and the cottonwood trees
knew they didn't belong up there   Never mind
that electrical towers asserted their rights
that coyote brush said the land was its own
that the ridge wanted fire and we did not
We weed whacked   cleared   cut down those pines   Never
mind
that we heard their cries in the night
though they never belonged up there   Never mind
that the frogs went away one day and so did we

The ancient ones who walked these lands
who made their arrows from coyote brush
knew not to make one's home on a ridge
for a ridge will insist on fire

Home is in a valley
by a river among cottonwoods
where once there was a river
                where frogs once sang in spring

                          Never mind

WILD GIRL OF PLEASANT HILL

Once this was somebody's
grandparents' farm   sweet
as Rebecca of Sunnybrook
do you remember?   How she skipped
among meadows with wildflowers
'til thrown like a sheep
to the ground
shorn of her corn   her hay

She's still here   that girl
You'll see her playing in the fountains
near Rotten Robbie's Gasoline
or herding her geese by the Chinese
All-You-Can-Eat Buffet
while cars zoom past on 680
in sight of the mountain

You'd think she'd be dead by now
after all the concrete poured
That girl is wild
as Rima   talks to the willows
to the birches
laughs aloud at the ducks
who have commandeered
the community
swimming pool

Old ecstatic
of trees
have you forgotten
Green Mansions   that slip
of a girl who first lit
                  the green fire?

BLACK DWARF

Black Mountain College 1945

Who came up with so fairy tale a name for you?
Once you housed my greenhorn parents
the upstairs poet   his toy trains   the library lady   and me

Did I roll down your sunny lawns? Did I learn about stairs
on your front porch   or up the long flight
to see the trains run?   Was there snow in the winter?

Did your windows let in summer's full foliage?
Do you remember my first step   first word   first mashed
banana? Did you protect my sleep? Did you practice magic

in the way of the little people?   Did you teach me to cast
the circle   call the directions?   Are my dreams inscribed
in your walls?   Did creatures from other realms visit

your ceilings?   Are you haunted by my parents' early love
my father's Well Tempered Klavier   my mother's Mozart
Divertimenti   by Roland Hayes singing   in your living room

that Old Pharoah should let our people go?

You   little house with the enchanted name
toadstool under which my whole world hatched

IN THE GARDEN

for Obie

In your new house   painted shades
of sunlight and sky   there are windows
that contemplate

summer hills   the bay
Your little brother clatters from playroom
to living room to kitchen over shining floors

You show me your garden   its secret
hiding places   the apricot
brimming with fruit and your own

personal apple tree   You give me a taste
of tart green fruit   We talk of death
my father's and that of Florence

the Great Dane   "She stopped breathing"
you tell me   "Did your father
stop breathing too? Why?"

You are not yet four
I pray that this house
with its filtered light

its many rooms that remember
other lives   will protect you   Long
may your parents and your brother

breathe   long may you taste
the fruit of both trees
in the garden

At the Inn of Placelessness

Our stories are sailing away
in an upside-down boat
while we sleep   No longer are we the ones

who live in a house on a ridge
make love under redwood beams
are visited by owls

nor are we those   who came to this pier
farthest point west   long ago
There are boys skateboarding off

the edge   There are fishermen
throwing their lines   Where have they gone
the hands   hips   lips of the ones

we used to be   at the Old Molina
Whale Watch   Agate Cove?   We climb the stairs
of the lighthouse   footsteps

behind us   look out at the rocks   where so many
ships have foundered   their well-crafted hulls
their masts   their captains'

sleeping quarters drift down
We look for ourselves
in the fire   Will the burning wood remember

how many grandfather   redwood trees
have shadowed our paths so a ray
could touch our heads?

Is there a counting angel who tallies it up
walks taken   beds slept in   love made?
Also the fights   bad blood   words burnt

in the mouth?   Is there an angel
who collects   every broken shard
who will write it all down?

SEA VOYAGE

From the first sea voyage in the body of my mother
from the sweet smell of her flesh   gush of her blood
light in her eyes   I have been lucky   Seas

carried me to Italia when I was a child   I heard the bells
smelled sunripe tomatoes   touched stories
on a golden door   Ruth
                    amidst the alien corn

Don't misunderstand   none of this has been easy
Sea voyages are perilous   the hard thrusting push
to get out of the family   out
of the wrong marriage   out
of a sluggish sleep

attracted many a sea monster   They ate me
for breakfast   spat me out at Ninevah
swallowed me up again
in the night   full
of harrowing dreams

Lucky I say   very lucky
to be swallowed   spat out
swallowed again
Lucky to be washed up on so many
beaches   a guest among elephants at sunset   a pilgrim
in a stone chariot   come only lately to where
I can rest   and contemplate
                              blue cosmos

Wet Lands

We began here
among the rushes
a slow sun rising behind Black Mountain

The little house on stilts remembers
Grandmother Fire and Flow
Grandmother Wet Lands   how she played
her clever hand

Your golden hair   a wilderness
until the age of parting
brushing   braiding so tight
it pulled the skin
around your eyes

while She   Old Woman of the Marsh
ran away with the baby

It's twilight   an osprey hovers
You watch his dive   the spray
of amazed waters   How long
do we still have?

Carnelian the light left
on Black Mountain   Carnelian
the dazzles
in the fast moving tide

The rushes know
light falls
to the bottom of things   light soars
like a hunting bird

and when it swallows you
perhaps you'll hear

                    your next life calling

About the Author

Naomi Ruth Lowinsky's poetry has been widely published. Her fourth poetry collection, *The Faust Woman Poems*, follows one woman's Faustian adventures during the 1960s and '70s, through Women's Liberation and the return of the Goddess. Her memoir, *The Sister from Below: When the Muse Gets Her Way* tells stories of her pushy muse. She is the author of *The Motherline: Every Woman's Journey to find Her Female Roots*.

Lowinsky is a Jungian Analyst and member of the San Francisco Jung Institute where she has taught a poetry workshop, *Deep River*, for many years. She is co-editor, with Patricia Damery, of the essay collection *Marked by Fire: Stories of the Jungian Way*. She is also Poetry Editor of *Psychological Perspectives*, a publication of the Los Angeles Jung Institute.

She lectures and gives writing workshops in many settings and blogs about poetry and life at sisterfrombelow.com.

www.ingramcontent.com/pod-product-compliance
Lightning Source LLC
Chambersburg PA
CBHW051742040426
42447CB00008B/1257